COMMENTS FROM READERS

I just wanted to comment on your brief words about life, lives, intersecting, listening. Wow. Those words were so clean and crisp to me, like fall in New Hampshire picking apples and sneaking that first juicy bite. Very distinct.
Louise, South Carolina

I'm writing you a quick note to let you know how much I enjoyed reading *Sacred Intersections*. You've brilliantly articulated many thoughts that I've pondered. The intersection analogy wonderfully connected a lot of the dots for me. It's a book I will recommend to others - and buy for each of my adult kids.
Bob, Ohio

I lead a new initiative called Theology on Tap. Several people gather monthly at a local pub to discuss life and spirituality. This diverse group of people is being prompted in our discussions by *Sacred Intersections*. Most recently we kicked around what it means to love our neighbor. Steve's notion that every encounter is a holy one guided us into commitments to be fully present to everyone we meet. This book is full of simple yet profound truth.
Kevin, Minnesota

Before reading *Sacred Intersections*, I found myself extremely unsatisfied with the way people stuffed God into a list of rules and Only One Certain Way of Doing It, into something they can control. I realized I'd spent practically my entire life trying to please a God who in no way cared about me trying to do the right thing or squeeze myself into this cookie-cutter shape people had convinced me that I was meant to look like. When I began trusting, instead of trying to please God, is when I noticed change. Small, mind you, and still very much in its infant stages, but nonetheless, I think it's there. I slow down in intersections, I'm more patient with people, genuinely care to hear their story. I feel like this little kid part of me—the part that looked around an airport as a 5-year-old and wondered about the people walking by, about their worries and their families and their thoughts and where they were going and why and where they came from—this part of me that I'd lost, this part that actually thought of others instead of myself all the time, I've finally found again. For the first time in my life, I feel as though I'm legitimately understanding what it is to trust God. And there is such freedom in that.

Sophie, Oregon

One of my favorite thoughts in *Sacred Intersections* is the very simple advice to "slow down in the intersections." Everyone gets "occupied" with their own stuff—dreams, fears, family, work, worries, etc. Our stuff consumes so much energy and leaves very little time for real reflection and interaction. We are so busy that we accelerate through the intersections. Steve Adams reminds us that vital decisions and discoveries are made at life's intersections. We must be alert and aware so we don't miss important markers and people on our journey.

Peter, California

To Pete,
May all your intersections
be enjoyable & enhancing!,

SACRED
INTERSECTIONS
enjoying and enhancing the stories around us

STEVE ADAMS

Thanks so much for your
wonderful hospitality. I love
your heart for the kingdom. I'm
grateful our stories have intersected.
All the best,

THREE FIVE SIX Press

Steve

Published in the United States by ThreeFiveSix Press.

www.sacredintersections.net

ISBN 978-0-9859750-0-5

Printed in the United States of America

To Linda, whose story is intertwined with mine
in all the fullness of love and sacredness

CONTENTS

STARTING POINT

There is a game I sometimes play. Often, I do it while waiting alone in a busy environment—an airport lounge, a crowded freeway, an auditorium before a concert. I take notice of someone else sitting nearby or walking past. Then I reflect on the fact there were countless decisions, experiences, and circumstances that brought that person to be in proximity with me at that moment, in that place. And then I consider that it was not only his own decisions and experiences that brought him here, but the decisions and experiences of his parents and grandparents and great-grandparents—multiple generations back to the beginning of time. All those factors brought him to this very moment in time, here, next to me. I marvel at the complexity of it all. Where he is at that precise point in time is the culmination of a very long story, and now his story is intersecting with my story and all its intricacies.

Mind boggling.

Should we just write it off to chance, this intersection of our stories? Or, is it possible that there is more to it if we just pay attention?

Sometimes, I stop the game there, and it ends up feeling like a purely random encounter. But sometimes I go further. And when I do, it becomes much more enjoyable. As I use the opportunity to appreciate and validate that person, it is no longer just a game. It becomes a sacred intersection.

PREFACE

This book is an invitation to a way of being.

In today's world, you don't have to look far to observe ways of being that don't seem to be working. Many of us feel like our lives are fragmented. Fear is often behind our decisions. Strained personal relationships are all too common. Global economic pressures bring out the worst in us. At a time when we need each other more, we seem to be less available—and less and less humane. Hope and joy are on the wane and cynicism on the rise, sadly evidenced by soaring drug abuse and suicide rates, especially among the young.

Our political institutions aren't providing the answers. Neither, would it seem, are our religious institutions. God is largely out of the conversation except when it's convenient to use him as a political pawn or for judgmental manipulation.

There is a way forward that can be different from all that. A way of being that is restorative and relational. A way of being that can reintegrate your life in connection with God, other people, and the rest of creation. A way of being that will make your life more enjoyable and more meaningful.

I invite you to take your time as you read about it in this book. Ponder it. Though the chapters are short, take the time to absorb and live out each chapter's ideas before moving on to the next one. Add your own stories to the ones written here, and in that way become a co-author with me in your unique living version of the book. And if you would like to share any of those stories, you can do so at www.sacredintersections.net.

Each chapter can stand alone, but there is an in-tended flow. I start with how sacred intersections play out for us as individuals and then move toward how they can be shared in community. One way of learning to live these ideas out in com-munity is to work through the book, one chapter at a time, with a group of friends. There is a guide for further reflection and discussion available on the website.

My hope is that in these pages you will discover some new questions and some fresh insights that will help you understand your own life story and enjoy more fully how it intersects with others' stories.

ONE: **MYSTERY**

[the gift of sacred intersections]

The longer I live the more I appreciate things that are profound, things I can't fully understand. At the heart of my appreciation is the freedom that comes from realizing there is much that is beyond me and many things I am unable to comprehend.

I can't fully explain why I am awestruck by snow-capped mountain peaks or enraptured by good jazz or melted by the laughter of a child. I don't fully know why I feel such satisfaction helping someone who is in need or why it feels so good to arrive home after a long trip. These things are mysterious to me, but that mystery only enhances my experience of them.

Admitting the mystery is a step of humility, which pushes me toward gratitude—the acknowledgement that what I have at that moment has been given to me. When I experience mystery in that way, I experience God in the midst of it.

Sensing God in the beauty and majesty of nature or the arts is nothing new. In fact, it's a pretty universal human experience.

Lately, however, I've been equally awestruck by the mystery of intersections. And experiencing that awe mostly depends on my own attitude and posture. When I allow myself to consider just how mysterious it truly is when I have an encounter with another human being, something happens: the encounter takes on a whole new level of meaning.

When I pause to think about the overwhelming complexity of choices and events that led to that moment of our two stories intersecting, I become more sensitized to the other person. I notice things I wouldn't otherwise notice. I'm more curious about how he or she arrived at this moment. I'm more willing to engage in conversation. I listen better and comprehend more. I'm more able to enjoy the uniqueness of the other person.

And it just feels sacred. Like a gift from God.

I recently met my good friend Thom for an after-work drink. He brought along another friend, a man who was an immigrant. Though I had briefly met this man before, I hadn't spent enough time with him to bridge the culture gap I sensed between us.

As we sat down, Thom asked the man to tell us the story of how he had come to be in the U.S. He was somewhat reluctant to begin, but with a little coaxing he launched into it. We sat spellbound as he told the story of being drafted into the military in his home country and subsequently being forced to carry out actions in a neighboring country that he knew were unjust. He went AWOL and escaped on a refugee boat, drifting for weeks at sea and finally landing in a refugee camp in yet another country. With little hope and no plan of getting out, he simply tried to make the best of it. The average time people spent there was about three months, but he was there over a year. Then, because he had shown some kindness to a single mother in the camp, when she was able to make her way into the United States, she took it upon herself to make the connections that led to his being able to get into the U.S. as well. He is now a successful entrepreneur, married with kids.

I could tell it was a story he had not told often. I felt honored to hear it and had a newfound respect for him. Suddenly the cultural distance between us seemed much less.

Amazingly, Thom, who had initiated the whole conversation, then remarked how there was an overlap between this man's story and his own. Thom's family had lived in the same country where the refugee camp was. While he was still in elementary school, they were forced to leave the country for religious/political reasons and moved to the United States. Both of his parents took on jobs that were well beneath their level back home, working long hours just to make ends meet. He recounted the challenges of those early years— the difficulty of adapting into a new context, the pain of not being accepted and being bullied. He talked of resenting his parents in his youth, but also of how as he moved into adulthood he gained a deep appreciation for the sacrifices they had made for him to have a better life.

This, too, was a story I had never heard before— and from someone I considered a good friend! To my shame, I had simply never inquired about it.

I sat there, basking in the feeling that this was a sacred place to be. I felt grateful and savored the moment.

It was a happy hour that lived up to its name.

Everybody has a story. Most of the time, I just don't pay attention to it.

TWO: **OCCUPIED**

[living in the moment]

Intersections are tricky places. More accidents happen in intersections than anywhere else on the road. You have to pay attention or you can get yourself into trouble. Generally, it's a good idea to slow down when entering one.

I'm one of those people who are habitually preoccupied. Even though it has been about 20 years since I was a professor, I still get accused of being an absent-minded one. I can very easily go along on a thought trail for an extended period of time with virtually no awareness of what's going on around me. (For some reason, my wife doesn't seem to like it when I do this and it's her words that are going on around me.)

Preoccupied. When you break the word into its two halves, you get *pre* and *occupied*—in other words, being occupied with something before you need to be. Doing so takes you out of the moment you're in, and the simple reality is that the moment you're in is the only reality that actually is. (Spend some time chewing on that one.)

You get the same net effect from being "post-occupied"—overly dwelling on the past in wistful fantasies or regretful "if only..." scenarios.

I recently added a standing item to my to-do list: "Be occupied." It serves as a reminder to me to live in the moment. To be aware. And to slow down in the intersections.

It's a difficult habit to develop, slowing down in the sacred intersections—those places where your story intersects with someone else's. There are so many easy, entertaining diversions that can occupy our attention; an iPod and headphones can be just the ticket to avoid any awareness. And, there are so many things to worry about: job or school stress, family pressures, financial concerns, health issues, environmental crises, wars. It's hard not to be preoccupied with it all. And then there's simple busyness, too often worn as a badge of honor in our culture. Saying yes to too many things and then scurrying around to get it all done is a sure-fire way to miss the sacredness of intersections.

But when I'm occupied with the moment I'm in—aware of what's going on around me, attuned to the stories I'm intersecting with, curious about those stories, willing to look past my initial judgments and assumptions and engage with those stories—then I begin to be aware of the sacredness of it all.

And I begin to lose myself, in the best sense of the phrase, my focus no longer solely on me.

At that point, it is not necessary to actually interact with those I encounter. Circumstances don't always allow for that. But I can turn my heart toward the people I come across. I can silently wish them well and pray for them. I can hope that whatever is burdening them would be eased. I can hope that they will find things to celebrate and enjoy. I can pray that God will guide them and bless them. It can all happen in a very short time.

I believe that such prayers can make a direct difference for someone. But even if they didn't make a direct difference, I'm convinced that my prayers would make an indirect difference, because when I pray for someone, it makes *me* different. And when I'm in a better place, it makes the world a better place. And that, ultimately, is good for those I'm praying for.

It is in that moment of turning my heart toward the other person that the intersection turns sacred, that I sense God in it, that I am changed. And I begin to find myself even as I lose myself.

Sometimes circumstances allow for interaction at the intersection. Maybe it's just a genuine smile that reflects your well wishes for the other person at that moment. If you have slowed down at the intersection enough, you might notice an opportunity to perform a simple act of kindness—holding a door open, allowing someone who is arriving at the same time to get in the grocery checkout line first, or helping someone lift a carry-on bag into the overhead compartment. Perhaps a more significant and demanding act of service is in order if you are able. Kindness played out, whether small or large, is visible proof to others and to yourself that you are living in the sacredness of the intersection.

Oftentimes a conversation happens at the intersection. A kind word can have much the same effect as a kind act. Both invite the other person to slow down in the intersection with you. It's amazing how an open, caring posture can take you past small talk and into storytelling. And it's at that level— when you get to listen to the story of the other— that the sacredness comes alive, even if time only allows for a small piece of their story.

The best way to move the conversation to the storytelling level is to ask a good open-ended question. Here are a couple of my favorites, as obvious as they are:

To get it started:

I'm curious; what's your story? How did you come to be here today?

To keep it going:

Can you tell me more about that?

And then, listen.* Really listen. Turn off your assumptions and judgments. Stay attentive. Listen for their joys. Listen for their sorrows. Try to feel what they're feeling and reflect it back to them. Don't seek to fix, just seek to understand. And, if invited to, share something of your story as well.

Enjoy the process of entering someone else's story. Pay attention to the wonder and privilege of it. Be grateful. You're on sacred ground.

Part of what makes it feel sacred is that there's risk involved. When a person shares her story she

---

* I feel like such a hypocrite writing about listening. I truly am not good at it. My mind constantly wanders. But, perhaps the up side of that is since I know I'm not good at it, I have had to think more about it than a more natural listener would.

puts herself on display, and in so doing, she gives power to the hearer. She cannot control how that power will be used.

The hearer can receive it as a gift, expressing gratitude, affirmation, encouragement, and care. Or the hearer can use it to discount, judge, tear down, and harm her.

When we slow down at an intersection, with a heart at peace and a heart that is for the other person, then we are in the place to use that power well. We can honor the sacredness of the moment and use it for the other's benefit.

My wife Linda and I recently attended a wedding. During the reception, I ran into Susanne, an acquaintance who was going through a divorce. I don't know her well and hadn't seen her in months, but in that moment my heart felt for her so I genuinely asked, "How are you doing?" Immediately, her eyes welled up with tears as she recounted a bit about the season she was in. "It's funny," she said, "that I'm being so emotional about it. We're pretty much done with the whole process now. I haven't cried in months. Thanks so much for asking and for listening. It's just nice to know that there are people who care." My simple act of asking a sincere question elicited a response that was helpful for her—and a privilege for me. It was a sacred intersection.

Molly, another acquaintance, was standing there listening in. She, too, must have felt the sacredness of it, because she went on to tell much of her own life story, including some details that she would have normally kept confidential. The level of trust that was evident in my conversation with Susanne gave her the confidence to share openly. It was an example to me of how slowing down in an inter- section can cause others to slow down with you.

Slowing down, living in the moment, and listening to others—these actions don't come naturally. In fact, more often than not, the natural impetus is just the opposite. And as we'll see in the next chapter, it's all about our propensity for categories.

THREE: **CATEGORIES**

[from judging to love]

In our modern world, we have been taught very well to think in categories. Too well, in many cases.

Categories can be useful tools. They give us a way to make complexity simpler and easier to comprehend. By analyzing, comparing, and categorizing, we gain a degree of control over the complexity. This can help us make associations, predictions, and judgments about things. We've become quite good at it, too. In fact, our brains are pretty much hard wired to categorize. We actually have to work hard to *avoid* doing it.

But then, we normally don't try to avoid it, since we generally like the feeling of being in control of things.

We must never forget, however, that categorizing is a form of simplification and that once we have simplified something, we are overlooking its uniqueness and mystery. There are some arenas that would do well with less categorizing.

Take people and their stories for instance. It's so easy to make snap judgments about people the first time I lay eyes on them. I let categories of gender and ethnicity and body type and age and clothing style and any number of other things jump right to the front of the queue and preload my mind with all kinds of assumptions about people before I've even heard one word of their story. I ignore all the mystery of their history—multiple generations of decisions and experiences—and convince myself that I've already got a very good idea of who they are, thank you very much.

It's insidious.

Why am I so prone to this judging? Why do I insist on validating myself at the expense of others, consciously and subconsciously, overtly and covertly? Where does that come from? And how do I get rid of it? (Because I really don't like it.)

The ancient story about the Beginning gives unexpectedly powerful insight into all this. As the story goes, God made humankind in his own image to be in relationship with him.* Adam and Eve had a relationship with him that could best be described as one of openness, dependence and trust. And he created for them an environment in which everything they needed was provided.

Their relationship with each other was also completely open and authentic. They were "naked and unashamed."

They were also given the freedom to make choices, with just one warning: don't eat from the Tree

---

* My use of male pronouns in reference to God throughout this book is not intended as a theological statement. It's merely a matter of convenience, based on the limitations of English to provide us with a personal pronoun that is trans-gender. I find it too clunky to avoid pronouns altogether, so I've decided to go with the traditional male usage, though in my mind, God transcends gender.

of the Knowledge of Good and Evil. In its fruit is death.

So along comes the temptation, a clever combination of lie and truth that gets them to ignore the warning. The lie: The fruit won't harm you. The truth: You will be like God. (We know that this part is truth, because God confirms it a bit later in the story.)

The ironic part is that they were already like God. They were made in his image, like God in ways that God wanted them to be like him.

Apparently, this knowledge of good and evil made them like God in a way that God never intended or desired. And the consequences were as advertised. Guilt, shame, deceit, blame, envy, even murder—all Hell literally breaks loose within a generation or two.

Death.

Lost is the quality of relationship they enjoyed with God.

Lost is their relationship of honesty and transparency with each other.

Lost is the harmony of their relationship with the rest of creation.

And, as a result of all that, lost is their sense of identity.

So much is lost. And the echoes of it still reverberate.

How does the knowledge of good and evil cause this? How does it make us like God in a way that we weren't designed for?

I think that the core of it is that it gives us the ability to make judgments. We can make pronouncements like "I'm right, you're wrong." "We're in, you're out." But we weren't designed for that, because we lack the perspective by which to make such judgments. Only God has that kind of perspective.

But the knowledge, once gained, is pervasive. We are compelled to create categories of what's right and what's wrong, along with categories of who's right and who's wrong. Our vain attempts to gain the necessary perspective to administer such categories and make judgments are just that: vain, in every meaning of the word.

We empower ourselves with delusions of objectivity and fairness. We create legal and religious institutions to help, but they, by nature, further depersonalize the process. Despite our best attempts, we're never up to the task. We can never fully see into the heart of things.

Judging pushes us away from relationship, away from other people. We seek the distance in an attempt to gain perspective. And in doing so, we place ourselves above them, looking down on them.

The whole process feeds the worst in us. It gives us powerful means to control others, and even when our initial motivations seem honorable, judging typically digresses into manipulation and coercion. We do it corporately and individually, and it results in hollow institutions and broken relationships.[*]

I can't even judge myself very well, much less anyone else.

I didn't choose to be born. I didn't choose when I was born or the family I was born into. I didn't choose my DNA, my basic attributes or aptitudes. All of that was handed to me, for better or for worse.

In addition to all of those things, a string of circumstances and experiences that prompted countless choices have mysteriously woven their way into the story of who I am—from my birth all the way up to the point that I now write this sentence. Equally mysterious is how others' choices have played into my story.

---

[*] I'm not advocating anarchy here. Nor am I unappreciative of the efforts of religious and civil servants who serve such institutions. I'm merely stating that all of our attempts to control a situation gone bad fall short of what we really need, and that if we actually lived as we were designed to be, we wouldn't need such solutions.

Sometimes I feel like a victim, other times responsible. Sometimes I feel blessed, other times a "blesser." Some of my choices seem to have been helpful, others destructive. Some of my motives have felt pure, others purely selfish. I'm no axe murderer, but neither am I Mother Teresa.

To be honest, I am unable to evaluate how well I have done at getting to this point in my life. And therein lies the problem. As long as I'm trying to judge myself in that way, I'm still stuck in the realm of the knowledge of good and evil.

I play comparison games: *Hey, at least I'm better than he is.* (Or the more subtle, but equally harmful, *I'll never be as good as she is.*) Or I measure myself against a standard—some code of ethics and conduct that allows me to feel righteous when I adhere to it, but leaves me feeling guilty when I don't.

This is where our religiosity comes from. We all know that something is wrong with the world and that a significant portion of what's wrong is because of our own doing. Therefore, most of us assume that God must be unhappy with us. In an attempt to make God happier with us, we look for a set of rules—the things we think really matter to God, based on our own intuitions, or religious books and teachers—then we hold ourselves and others to those standards. We figure that if we get good enough, God will accept us.

But it never actually works. The problem is that when we approach it this way, we're still operating out of our knowledge of good and evil. We mistakenly think we're in control of things because we can define and measure it all. But at some point we end up at an impasse, because we don't all agree on which definition of "goodness"—and how much of it—will make God happy.

We end up in broken relationships, and get trapped trying to convince ourselves that we're right and tell others that they're wrong. We hang out with people who agree with us and disassociate with those who don't—all in the name of God. And over time, we break into more and more factions because we find increasingly minor points over which to disagree and divide.

We convince ourselves that if we can get everyone on the same page—if we'd all just think alike and talk alike and dress alike and act alike—*then* we will get along and do what's "right" (according to our group's definition). And on one level, this uniformity sort of works, at least for a while, giving the feeling that you are getting along and doing what's right.

But history tells us that as more and more people get into such a group, it becomes easier and easier for them to convince themselves that they're right and everyone else is wrong—and that God is on their side. Which means that God must be against everyone else. And then they gradually bridge into acting as agents of God's judgment, first by coercing and controlling those who are already in the group to stay that way, and then by imposing their way on others as they gain the power to do so.

Sometimes it leads to people doing extremely ugly things in the name of God.

If we view the Divine through the lens of the knowledge of good and evil, we are compelled to use legal, judgmental terms when we try to describe God. At the end of the day, if we're honest with ourselves, we all realize that we're guilty of some infractions in our lives that leave us short of the perfection of a holy God. And so we either strive to clean up our act in order to somehow appease him, or we blow it all off and deny he exists or at least mentally and practically put him at a safe, non-involved distance.

But what if God doesn't want us using the knowledge of good and evil the way we do? Remember, it was he who warned us to stay away from it in the first place.

What if his desire for the world is to restore "what was lost" in the story of the Beginning? What if we were to assume that somehow he has found a way to look past our shortcomings and view us with grace and love and forgiveness? What if God is actually for us and not against us? What if he is inviting us back into a relationship of openness, dependence and trust?

And what would it look like if we joined him in all that? What if, instead of uniformity, we sought unity—the kind of unity that is fueled by appreciation of diversity? What if we practiced grace and love and forgiveness with each other?

What if we lived as if God actually loves us?

All of us.

What if?

That's what I'm trying to explore and encourage with this book. But I have to say, it's not as easy as it sounds. That knowledge of good and evil is pretty deeply embedded in our psyches. And we have millennia of political, cultural, and religious systems that are built on it.

But, when we accept God's love—his unconditional, restore-what-was-lost love—and then extend it to each other, it moves us beyond the knowledge of good and evil. If I trust that God loves me, then I'm free to love myself, which in turn frees me to love others. And when I remember that God loves others in the same way he loves me, it changes how I view and interact with them.

Living as if God actually loves us changes everything.

The challenge of love is that it is not so easily defined and it requires us to relinquish control.

I can't force you to love me. I *can* force you to do things for me that might make it look like you love me, but I can't change your heart toward me. I can simply love you and invite you to love me in return.

That's the risk. You may choose not to love me.

I'm okay with that risk, because even if you choose not to love me, it doesn't change the sacred experience I have when I take the risk of loving you. The risk of loving is the most powerful act of faith there is.

FOUR: **FAMILIARITY**
[trust, honesty, grace]

Our enjoyment of a sacred intersection is heightened when the circumstances around it seem random to us. We take pleasure in the serendipity, saying, "I could NEVER have planned this! This really feels like God orchestrated it." And that is a reasonable response.

But is an intersection actually any less sacred when we can trace some of the choices that led to it? Is the mystery of multiple generations of decisions and experiences actually diminished when people make a conscious effort to make an intersection happen? If an intersection is scheduled into my calendar, does it mean that God is less interested or involved in it when it happens?

When we have an ongoing relationship with another person—when our stories become intertwined—it's easy to begin to take things for granted. As the saying goes, familiarity breeds contempt. Or, in the present context, familiarity easily steals away our awareness of the sacred in our intersections.

I often treat the people I'm closest to in ways that I wouldn't treat a perfect stranger. I'm short with Linda. I bark at my kids. I'm slow to reply to an e-mail from a good friend.

I regularly need to remind myself that my interactions with those familiar to me are sacred intersections like any other. I need to slow down, be occupied, and enjoy them. But there's a deeper dimension to it than that.

On top of the normal mystery of any intersection, there's another even more profound mystery: that someone who has had one intersection with me would choose to have another. And another. And another.

It is astonishing and humbling.

When two people intentionally approach every encounter with each other as a sacred intersection, it creates a cumulative effect that is powerful and profound. Trust develops.

Trust is like a commodity, and it grows in direct proportion to the risk invested in establishing it.

Every time someone takes the risk to share something of his or her story, and the recipient responds with love and grace, trust is formed. As trust forms, it compels a greater degree of risk— a willingness to reveal more and more of the story. And when that risk-trust dynamic is mutual, a healthy relationship can continue to grow indefinitely.

The pace at which this happens varies, but one thing is certain: trust is much more quickly destroyed than it is formed. A single lie, a single belittling comment, a single breach of confidentiality can undo months or even years of trust-building. And when it happens, the person who feels betrayed becomes more callous and hesitant to re-enter the risk-trust dynamic, not only with the betrayer, but with others as well. If it happens enough times, that callousness can become difficult to break through. We all know people who have a history of hurts that hinder them from engaging in healthy, trusting relationships.

That is not to say that there isn't room in a trusting relationship for honest feedback. In fact, the greater the degree of trust that is formed, the greater the level of authenticity and transparency that is possible. We all have our blind spot issues. When we have enough trust in another to invite his or her honest feedback, we can receive that input as a gift and use it to grow. Even if it hurts. It's the blind spots that keep us from being all that we were made to be, so receiving input that can help us address those things is a gift indeed.

One word of caution: honest feedback will be best received when it is invited. Unsolicited input can easily be received as an attack that undermines trust rather than building on it. The best way to create a willingness in others is to model it yourself by seeking their input and graciously receiving it.

The people I know who are most able to enter into the risk-trust dynamic at that level are those who are self-aware enough to admit their own foibles. They are humble. And if they have expressed that humility to God, trusting in his love and grace in response to their own authenticity, then something deep in their soul happens. Their sense of self is enlivened. There is internal joy and peace. And, there is an incredible sense of freedom—the kind of freedom where they can get their eyes off of themselves and on to others. If you truly believe that God loves you, then many fears begin to disappear, including the fear of rejection by other people.

A few years ago I had some colleagues give me their honest feedback. They were observing some things in me that were hindering me both personally and professionally, centered on patterns of defensiveness and excuse-making. Since I was largely blind to it, it was difficult to hear, but I chose not to dismiss it.

Instead, I decided to do some soul searching and see if I could get to the bottom of it. Based on the feedback I received, it seemed to me that there must be some underlying factor causing the behaviors they observed. It just wasn't apparent to me at first. I knew I needed a concentrated block of time to reflect on it all.

A good friend had offered me the use of his vacation home on a lake in the mountains any time I wanted it. So, I called him and headed up there by myself for a couple of days. The five-hour drive gave me ample time to unwind. I intentionally left the car audio system off and simply tried to clear my mind of all worries and distractions. One thought kept coming to the forefront as I drove along: I was grateful to God for all the good things in my life. By the time I reached my destination, I had thought of so many things I was grateful for, I was almost overwhelmed by it. I stood there looking out at the lake feeling drenched in God's grace. That night as I went to bed, I knew my heart was in a good place.

The next morning, I set my mind to the task at hand. I pulled out my notes on the input I had been given. I thought about each point, looking back over my life and considering if and how the feedback was valid. After a couple of hours, I still wasn't having any breakthroughs; I was not seeing any connecting points that brought deeper insight.

I decided to take a break and get outside in hopes that it would help. It was a beautiful spring day. I decided to drive further up into the mountains to hike the trail to a waterfall I knew would be flowing well at that time of year. In the 30 minutes or so of driving, I think I only passed one car. When I arrived at the trailhead, no other cars were in the parking lot. During the mile-and-a-half hike, I didn't see anyone. I knew I was as alone as I could get.

As I arrived at the base of the falls with the mist hitting my face, I was struck by the beauty that surrounded me. But I was still feeling stuck in my process. I was being as honest with myself as I could, and it wasn't working. Inwardly, I knew that what I really wanted was to hear from God about it. So, I found myself saying out loud, "OK, God. I am here to listen. Speak." And then I added with a slight chuckle, "But you've got to speak up, because these falls are loud."

What followed was one of the most remarkable experiences of my life. Immediately, completely out of nowhere, came an answer into my mind that was so clear I'm still not sure if it wasn't physically audible. The tone of voice was almost matter-of-fact.

"When I created this place, I had this day in mind, to enjoy it with you."

I was stunned. I literally gasped for air. I was completely undone. The implications of the statement were beyond my comprehension.

And then, in my deepest place of being, there welled up a joy that was so pure and so intense that it was overwhelming. I felt almost giddy and started dancing around on the rocks at the base of the falls.

Spontaneously, I put my hands up around my mouth and yelled out, "I love God!" I felt free in a way that I had never felt free before, and an even more intense wave of joy engulfed me. I did it again, even louder: "I LOVE GOD!"

More freedom. More joy. Gratitude filled my heart.

I'm still not sure how long this state of euphoria lasted, but after a while I caught myself and realized that I wanted to get everything I had experienced into my journal. So I sat and wrote it all down.

In doing so, the euphoria matured into a profound sense of well-being. Though for many years I had sought a close and personal relationship with God, never before had I had such a real sense of his love. I was aware that something had changed deep within me, but at the moment I simply wanted to relish the love I was feeling. Which is what I did for the rest of that afternoon and evening.

The next morning I woke up, immediately reminded of the previous day. I was still very aware of God's love toward me, and a spontaneous "I love you" to him was on my lips.

I sat down with the list of comments I had received from my colleagues, ready to consider once again what was there. Quite quickly I saw an underlying pattern to the feedback. My defensiveness, my excuse making, my self-justification mechanisms, and even what some people perceived as my arrogance were all reflections of a deeper motivation. I was driven by fear based on the question, "What will people think?"

I could see it consistently played out in my life choices and in my relationships. My drive to achieve was based on it. I was noncommittal at times because of it. ("I don't want to be overly associated with so-and-so, because *what will people think?*") In other circumstances, I would oversell something I was affiliated with, because my own sense of identity (based on what other people think) was wrapped up in it.

I had even done it with God. In my teen years I had begun seeking God, but I had always held back a part of me, again for fear of what others might think if I was too fanatical or something.

As I thought about this last point, it hit me that this is what had broken free the previous day. I knew that what I had experienced was a gift from God—a very special expression of his love for me. And my spontaneous response had been to reflect that love back to him wholeheartedly, without any reservation. I remembered that as I yelled "I LOVE GOD" I had an accompanying wish that someone would be coming down the trail toward the falls and hear me. I wanted to tell someone what I had just experienced and how amazing God is. I had no fear of being associated with God at all; in fact, I felt just the opposite.

That retreat in the mountains was a few years ago now, but I still get moved when I think about it. Ever since, I have been more consistently confident in God's love for me, regardless of circumstances I encounter or mistakes I make along the way. (Don't miss the point that it was while I was honestly examining my own shortcomings that God spoke to me with such love and affirmation.) Gradually, I have become less and less concerned about what others think of me, which has been so freeing. I have been changed by it.

Although God's expression of love to me on that spring day was special, I am realizing that he could say something similar to me every day if I was listening. If he exists and if he is truly a loving God, then it is no stretch to imagine him anticipating every day and every moment of every day as an opportunity to enjoy it with me.

And with every other person on the planet.

When I practice that kind of familiarity with God—when I am aware of his grace and love for me—I am free to live openly and authentically and to pass that love on to others in sacred intersections. It's a taste of the "naked and unashamed" that was the description of the man and woman before they ate of the Tree of Knowledge of Good and Evil.

Grace fosters trust, which allows for increasing honesty and transparency, which leads to growth, which increases our capacity to extend love and grace, which fosters trust....

And around and around it goes, unless something happens to break that cycle....

FIVE: **CRASHES**

[blame and forgiveness]

My wife, Linda, has the privilege of using a car leased by the company she is affiliated with. Every few years we have to take a defensive driving class in order to comply with their insurance program. Over and over again, the instructors stress the importance of being aware of what is going on around you, especially when entering an intersection. "You can only control what you do, not what anyone else is doing," they say. They give tips like, "Wait a couple of seconds after a light turns green before you go, since there are often people who speed through an intersection even after their light has turned red."

And, of course, they tell lots of stories (and often show gruesome photos) of what can happen if you aren't careful.

I don't want to push the analogy too far, but there is a degree to which this kind of thinking applies to the idea of sacred intersections. Especially the part about what you can and can't control.

A significant dimension of living in the sacredness of intersections is the art of discerning what's going on with those around you so that crashes can be avoided. Sometimes it's patently obvious when another person is not in a good place for an intersection. Maybe they're in such a busy mode that the best thing you can do for them is to stay out of the intersection. Just let them pass on through, and silently wish them well as they go.

Perhaps the person you're about to intersect with is under a lot of stress or having a particularly bad day. In such cases, it sometimes helps to gently edge into the intersection a little. A consoling word or act of kindness, if they will receive it, might be just what they need to adjust their speed—which just might help them avoid a more serious crash with someone else later in the day.

Then there are those people who live life as if it were a demolition derby, quite willing to crash into anyone who gets in their way. This attitude might show up as anger, manipulation, addiction, selfishness, or abusiveness, but at the root of it for most of these people is the feeling of being a victim.

Dealing well with such people goes beyond the scope of this book, but I do have a couple of general thoughts on the subject. First, remember that they typically have stories that are filled with pain. Considering their struggles can help explain how these unhealthy behaviors have emerged in their lives. Knowing this can help keep your heart turned toward them, hopeful for them, helpful if possible, while at the same time maintaining boundaries that will prevent them from crashing into you. It doesn't do you any good if they crash into you, and it doesn't do them any good either. Too often, especially in cases of abusive behavior, the abuser is allowed to continue in his or her destructive patterns by those who think it helps them to allow the abuse. It doesn't. Though we can't control someone else's choices, each of us can control our own. Sometimes the best thing we can do for another is to keep them from crashing into us.

But what about when we are the cause of a crash ourselves?

A few years ago, a friend of mine was driving in a downtown area of a small town at dusk. He was heading toward the sun, which inhibited his vision. He wasn't driving too fast or recklessly, but as he made a left turn across the road, a car coming the other direction suddenly became visible. It was too late to avoid a crash.

Both were going slowly enough that there was only minor damage to the vehicles. Unfortunately, there was an elderly woman riding in the other vehicle who wasn't feeling well after the accident. They took her to the hospital where, shockingly, she died shortly thereafter. It turns out that she had a congenital weakening of her aorta and the jolt of the accident, though not severe, was just enough to cause a tear.

My friend wasn't cited for the woman's death. It was determined that the collision was too minor to have caused an injury under normal conditions. But he has carried the weight of regret ever since.

The reality is, we don't know what state another human being might be in when we intersect with his or her story. Sometimes even a seemingly small misstep on our part can prove to be harmful.

Most of us can remember incidents when we have made a comment about someone intended in jest, only to find that person deeply hurt by it. Humor can be tricky that way. Your bumper-car banter may be someone else's head-on collision.

There are also times when I find myself causing crashes because, simply put, I'm being selfish. That other person becomes an obstacle in the way of me getting what I want.

I've been discovering that it's when I lose touch with the sacredness of my intersections that I am most prone to this. And interestingly, the way I lose touch with the sacredness is by losing touch with the humanity of the other person.

When I slip into the trap of categorizing people, as I talked about in Chapter 3, I find myself doing things or saying things that I usually regret. It can be so easy to allow a label—some stereotype or judgmental view—to take hold. And once I do, I project all this extra stuff that comes along with the label on to that person, even when I haven't actually observed any of it. I hear what they say through the filter of that label, and I interpret what I see in their behavior through the lens of that label.

Picture this scene (an imaginary compilation of somewhat similar experiences I've had): I walk into a busy restaurant with a colleague for a business meeting over breakfast. We are seated at a table, and a waitress approaches to take our order. She seems a little scattered, and she has a fairly thick foreign accent. It's difficult to understand her, but we manage to give her our order. We roll our eyes at each other as she scurries away. A few minutes later she arrives with our food, but part of the order is wrong. We point out the problems to her, and after she leaves to make the corrections, we exchange comments about her not being the sharpest pencil in the box and how it's hard to find good help these days. I make a mental note to go on the low side with the tip.

A couple of tables away is a man with three young children. The man is looking over some papers, not paying any attention to the kids, who are being squirrelly and loud. They are becoming a distraction, and we are not appreciating the interruptions to our important conversation. The dad looks up and sees us glaring at him. He mutters something to the kids to settle down and then buries himself again in his reading. We comment to each other that he's probably a single dad who's too busy for his kids when it's his turn to have them. "If he can't handle his kids, he shouldn't bring them in here!"

The next time I glance over at the man, I see him conversing with the waitress. She points at one of his papers and explains something to him. I can see the stress in his face easing just a bit. She then heads over to our table, and thinking out loud says, "That poor man..."

"What's wrong?" we ask.

"He's been up all night at the hospital. He just picked up his kids from his sister's house, because she had to leave for work. His wife was taken by ambulance to the hospital last night after passing out. They're still not sure what's wrong. He said he was confused by the medical reports, so I took a look to see if I could help."

"Huh?" we say.

"Before I moved here, I was doing a medical residency in my home country. It got cut short because my husband and I had to leave to seek political asylum. It will be a long process before I will be allowed to practice medicine here. But at least I was able to help that man with one thing that he didn't understand. Oh...and I'm sorry about the mistake with your order earlier. One of our cooks and one of our waitresses both called in sick at the last minute, so we're scrambling a bit. I should have caught it, though."

Knowing more of the story changes everything.

How quick we can be to attach labels, and how wrong we can be in our assumptions.

How easy it is to view someone as less than a fully equal human being who is made in the image of God—a person with a story and needs and desires that are just as valid as my own.

When I view people as less, I then feel justified in treating them in ways that are less than how I would want to be treated. My heart is no longer for them. Instead, at that point, I have actually turned things around and am blaming them for my poor behavior, because now, in my mind, they deserve to be treated that way.

The more I justify myself, the more strongly I attach the label, which causes me to further justify myself. It's a vicious cycle.

The cycle can start when I use a label to categorize someone and then feel justified to treat him badly. Or, it can start when I treat someone badly and then assign the label as a way to justify the way I treated him. In either case, I get caught in the cycle.*

It can happen with a sales clerk. It can happen with a neighbor. It can happen with a business associate. It can happen with a spouse.

And as far as I can tell, the only way out of the cycle isn't for the other person to change. It's for me to change. To recalibrate. To recognize what I'm doing and remind myself of the sacredness of intersections. To remove the labels and assumptions I use (in other words, stop judging), and turn my heart toward the other. At that point, I'm no longer causing a crash, and am, in fact in a position to help repair any damage that was done.

---

* The dynamics of this cycle are brilliantly discussed in two books published by the Arbinger Institute: *Leadership and Self-Deception*, and *The Anatomy of Peace*. I highly recommend both.

There are always at least three entities impacted in a relational crash. The first two are the individuals who run into each other, and the third entity is the relationship that exists between them. (Sometimes, of course, there are other relationships and individuals that are impacted as well.)

To whatever degree a person is at fault in a crash, the repair to his own personhood is his responsibility. The healing begins when he fully admits fault, expresses regret to the other person involved, and seeks forgiveness.

As for the other person—the one wronged in the crash—the only path to his personal restoration is forgiveness.

The third dimension, the relationship itself, can only be repaired when both of those personal dimensions are done—with honest regret on the one hand and forgiveness on the other. And, depending on how deep the relationship was and the severity of the crash, it may be relatively easy to pick up where you left off. Or it may take a long period of rebuilding trust for the relationship to get back to a healthy place.

Given that the knowledge of good and evil resides within us, it is not easy to admit our faults or to offer forgiveness. We have to work against our propensity to control things in order to do so. To admit a mistake and ask for forgiveness is to put the other person in control of the relationship. It does not, however, put them in control of you. In admitting fault and seeking forgiveness, you are restoring your own soul. At that point, the response of the other person has no power over you. You are free to turn your heart toward them and be at rest in your own soul, regardless of how they respond.

Only the relationship itself is at risk at that point. And it's important to note that the previous level of relationship was already lost when the crash occurred. By asking for forgiveness, you are not risking anything that isn't lost already. If the other person forgives you, then the relationship can move forward again. If not, then things merely remain where they already are. You may feel grief at the loss of the relationship, but the wellness of your own soul isn't lost.

Likewise, offering forgiveness is a personal choice that leads to freedom and wholeness in your own soul. On that level, it is independent of the other person involved. Unforgiveness, even if it feels "justified," actually doesn't have any direct impact on the other person. It only gnaws away at you. If the other person doesn't admit any fault and hasn't sought forgiveness, withholding forgiveness doesn't do you any good. In fact, at that point you have made your own sense of well being dependent on them. You have no control over whether or not they will ever admit to anything or accept any responsibility. Instead of having power over them, you have given them power over you! You have made yourself into a victim and a slave to their choices.

Withholding forgiveness from people who *have* admitted their fault and asked for forgiveness has the same net effect. Their own sense of well-being isn't determined by whether or not you offer them forgiveness. So, withholding forgiveness from them will only cause bitterness in you. Many people carry a grudge—sometimes for years and years—thinking that in some way they are hurting or harming the other person. The reality is, they are only harming themselves. With forgiveness comes freedom.

One last thing on crashes: In most crashes, both parties have some degree of fault, equal or not. Healthy restoration requires both individuals to completely acknowledge their own part in causing the crash and also to fully forgive the other's part in it.

SIX: **ANTICIPATION**

[life as a treasure hunt]

In January of 2010, a 7.0 earthquake hit the nation of Haiti. In what was already the poorest country in the western hemisphere, the effects were devastating. Homes and public buildings, many of which were built below typical modern standards, were pulverized. Nearly a quarter of a million people died, and hundreds of thousands of the survivors were left without shelter.

I work for a non-profit agency that encourages and facilitates the kinds of things I'm talking about in this book. Although we are not typically a relief organization, because of some contacts we already had in Haiti we decided to join with a few other organizations to facilitate a team of first-responders. Ten days after the quake, we were in Haiti with several doctors, nurses, EMTs, crisis counselors, and general helpers. It was both one of the most sobering and one of the most meaningful experiences of my life.

Imagine a mountainous pile of concrete chunks that were once a multi-story building, the nose of a barely recognizable vehicle sticking out, and the sickening realization that in that rubble and maybe in that pancake of a car are bodies that once carried the souls of employees and clients, mothers and fathers, friends and neighbors, artists, educators, accountants, and children—so many lovely, productive image-bearers of God lost to this generation in Haiti. Confronted with such horror, my personal impulse was to retreat into numbness. But each turn of the head, each glance in a new direction, would bring a fresh assault. It was impossible to retreat given the magnitude of the destruction.

The other impulse was to be overwhelmed by it all. Thousands upon thousands of buildings were destroyed or seriously damaged, and much of the infrastructure was debilitated. Clearly it will take years and years to rebuild, and the collective grief and loss of irreplaceable human potential are beyond imagination.

With numbness pulling one way and the feeling of being overwhelmed pulling the other, we managed our way forward by approaching things one person at a time, as we had the opportunity. Our doctors treated hundreds of patients of all ages, some with life-threatening medical issues, some with less serious but painful injuries, and all wanting the reassurance that comes from a professional diagnosis and treatment plan. In addition, our team talked and prayed with hundreds more, seeking to bring some measure of hope and healing to the emotional and spiritual side of things, too.

I will forever remember the sacred intersections I experienced in Haiti. I arrived home feeling grateful for having helped some people in dire need, and eager to continue with a long-term restoration strategy in Haiti.

A month later, we were pulling together another team. This time, in addition to medical assistance, we were focused on providing food and shelter. I invited my friend, Neal, to join us.

Neal is a successful international banker. He happened to be between jobs at that point in his life, so I knew he was available. And, he speaks French, which is one of the official languages of Haiti. He had never done anything quite as dramatic or as risky as volunteering to help in a severe disaster area. After discussing the potential risks with his wife, he agreed to come, sensing that it was the right thing for him to do.

During that week, our team provided food to about 700 families, gave away 250 family-sized tents, and medically treated about 400 people. The combination of Neal's caring personality and language skills proved very helpful to the team. He especially enjoyed connecting with the Haitian children. In fact, they captured his heart. He said that he had never felt more alive.

Our last stop before leaving Haiti was to visit an orphanage that we had some connections with. We were there to find out how we could help them in the future. In that orphanage, Neal met a 17-year-old boy named Mario. They had a true, sacred intersection, instantly building a bond of connection.

After arriving back home, Neal began corresponding with Mario and with the orphanage's director. Ever since, he has been an advocate for the good work that this orphanage is doing. And, his relationship with Mario has become a very important part of his life. Though there is significant geographical and cultural distance between them, Neal provides him with a fatherly perspective, encouraging him in his education and life goals. Mario in turn calls him "Daddy" and welcomes his involvement in his life. It's a wonderful thing.

Neal has since returned to Haiti three times with other teams, and has even recruited others to get involved. Haiti has become a central point of meaning and passion for him. And, in addition to personally touching the lives of many Haitians, his efforts have played a huge part in establishing a new, well-stocked medical clinic in an area where there has never been one. He is quick to say that he gets far more out of his involvement in Haiti than what he puts in. That's the nature of these kinds of sacred intersections.

And all because he took the risk to pursue an opportunity to make a difference for some people in need. He stepped out of his comfort zone.

When we choose to intentionally seek out sacred intersections in contexts that are outside of our norm, especially in situations that seem risky, we become more attuned to our dependence on God in the midst of these intersections. And thus, the enjoyment and meaning that we derive from them are heightened, and invariably things happen that have the fingerprints of God on them. Events fall into place that you could never have planned for. Conversations have a far greater impact on someone's life than you might have expected, because the right words just came to you. The resources that somebody needs become available in an unexpected way. A barrier to something good that you're planning is suddenly removed, for no apparent reason.

I've seen it time and time again, not only in my own life but in the lives of countless others.

And you don't have to do something as dramatic as a trip to Haiti for it to happen, although I do highly recommend such activities. It can happen anytime and anywhere that you're paying attention to the opportunities for sacred intersections around you. Take the risk to step out of your comfort zone—even if it only feels like a small step—for someone else's sake. When you do, then good stuff—God stuff—just seems to happen. It can bring a freshness to even the most mundane circumstances.

When I approach my day with an attitude of availability to God to engage in whatever sacred intersections he might send my way, that day becomes like a treasure hunt.

In her waning years, my maternal grandmother slid into fairly severe dementia. Fortunately, it was not the cantankerous kind. If anything, her sweet spirit was heightened. As it progressed and she was no longer capable of living on her own, my mother and father brought her into their home.

One morning, about a year into this living arrangement, Granny worked her way down the stairs and shuffled into the kitchen, where Mom was enjoying a cup of coffee. Upon seeing my mom, she exclaimed with a joyful expression, "Why Gene! You're the last person I expected to see *here!*"

I want to approach each day with that same perspective. I want each intersection—be it with my wife or with a perfect stranger—to enliven me with a sense of joyful anticipation.

SEVEN: **VOCATION**

[integrating your whole world]

Vocation is a word that has lost its luster in the modern era. The Latin root of the word is the same as our English words "voice" and "vocal." The implication is that vocation carries with it a sense of "calling" based on that which was spoken into your life by God himself. It refers to everything that makes you you—your unique blend of attributes, talents, perspectives, skills, and experiences. Fulfillment comes as you increasingly understand and develop all that was spoken *into* your life, and learn how to profess it, or speak it *out* of yourself, into your "profession." (Profession is another word that could use a facelift.)

With this understanding of profession, your work (whether it is formal, for-pay work or not) becomes an act of generosity—a process of giving away what was given to you—and thus it takes on a whole different level of meaning and enjoyment. It's a different form of sacred intersection, one in which your work is done with God for the benefit of others. And the more your work reflects what was poured into you, the more pleasurable it is and the less chance you have of burnout.

And the more integrated your life becomes.*

If you're the one giving it away, then you own your work, rather than it owning you. (Think about that one for a minute.)

My brother-in-law is a retired Postal Service employee. For several years, he served as the postmas-

---

* There are numerous self-assessment tools that can help you better know and understand what has been poured into you. One that I particularly recommend is The StrengthsFinder, which is an online tool published by the Gallup Organization. Passkey codes to take the test are included with several of their publications about it. Knowing your own strengths as well as the strengths of your coworkers can greatly enhance and enliven the workplace.

ter in a small town in northern California. Because of the rural nature of the area, many of the residents came in to the post office to pick up their mail. Pretty much everybody in the area got to know him, and he knew all of them.

Though professional and efficient, he also has a great sense of humor and a disarming way of connecting with people. Day after day, he not only ran the post office effectively, he also enjoyed his interactions with people and genuinely cared about them. His personal goal was that no one would leave the post office grumpy—even during the holiday season when lines get long and people's patience grows thin. For him, this was clearly a vocation.

When he announced his retirement, the whole town got together to throw him a farewell party. They presented him with a book of personal notes, summed up well by this entry: "I realize that I haven't come into the Post Office near enough in the years you have been here—to see you, your smile, your wit. Now that you will be gone, I will miss you. You are a unique and gifted human being, and all of us who have come under your spell have truly been blessed!"

The richness of these concepts of vocation and profession is lacking in the prevailing perception of a "job." A job is a set of tasks to be done, whether or not the person doing them is well suited to them or finds any joy or meaning in them. If the tasks get done, then the company or institution is satisfied. This arrangement is primarily defined by the needs of the company, which makes perfect sense, since it's the company that is paying to have that job done.

Thankfully, many companies and organizations now not only hire the people who best fit their jobs, but also figure out how to adjust their jobs to fit the best people. The most empowering scenario is when both the company and the individual view the role as a vocation.

Equally important is how the company itself operates. Is there integrity, both internally and externally? Are people and their families valued and not perceived as just another commodity to use up in the pursuit of higher production? Is the company environmentally responsible? Does it encourage community service?

It also helps when there is more than just a dollar sign at the bottom line—when a company or organization sees itself as providing goods or services that enhance people's lives and make the world a better place. While this is true of many companies, there is a new wave of businesses being established around the world that take it a step further. For them, corporate profit is truly a secondary concern. These "social enterprises" exist to do such things as provide jobs for as many poor or marginalized people as possible, create useful products out of waste that would otherwise pollute, train young business leaders to be released into an emerging economy, apply affordable renewable energy solutions in the developing world, and so on. For them, making a profit is still important, but it isn't the highest priority.

I am inspired by some young social entrepreneurs who are in the process of launching a plastic recycling plant in Haiti that will work in connection with a new drinking water bottling facility. Plastic waste is littered throughout the country and affordable clean drinking water is always in short supply. (In one of the villages where we have done medical clinics, the doctors report that more than 80% of the cases they are treating are directly related to bad drinking water.) This innovative new venture will address both of these major issues while also employing many Haitians who are currently out of work.

I am equally inspired by another new venture in South America that is currently in the planning stages. Their goal is to "upcycle" an agricultural waste product. Instead of disposing it in the typical, polluting way, they will use this waste product to make affordable building panels for low-income housing.

When the company you work at is socially aware, environmentally conscious, and values its people, it's relatively easy to turn a job into a vocation. But what about a work environment that is less altruistic? What about those places where there is little, if any, consideration for such matters?

Ultimately, it's up to the individual to determine his or her posture about work. You don't need to lower your own standards to match a workplace that is less than ideal. (To do so is to allow yourself to be a victim.) Your company may view you as merely a hireling in a job, but that doesn't have to stop you from approaching your role as a sacred vocation. Doing so may prove to be the very thing that brings about change in your workplace.

That is not to say that the workplace environment doesn't matter. It does. If you find yourself at odds with the goals or ethos of your workplace—if, from your perspective, it lacks integrity, is abusive or exploitative to its employees or customers, or provides products or services that are harmful—then it becomes a moral dilemma to give yourself generously into it, because you are helping to perpetuate things you disagree with. If changing it from within is not possible, then you might need to consider seeking another place of work.

Or create a new one. There's plenty of room out there for entrepreneurs who will lead the way in establishing fresh, new companies that are socially and environmentally conscious. The world needs more businesses that recapture the sacredness of vocation.

Making your work a vocation is, in itself, a form of sacred intersection. Giving of yourself in your work acknowledges God and benefits others.

Yet, if you're like most people, the workplace is also where you most regularly intersect with others. Approaching your interactions with coworkers and customers as sacred intersections can bring you more meaning and enjoyment, and can also enhance your performance on the people side of your work. It happens as you stay occupied and remain sensitive to the way people are entering those workplace intersections. Practice patience with a difficult coworker. Go the extra mile for a client, even when he is being annoying. Be respectful toward a boss, even if she is in a bad mood. Listen with understanding during a coffee break to a coworker who is having personal struggles outside of work. Actively participate in workplace social functions so you can be present and available.

Most of us who live in the western world, have been taught—either directly or indirectly—to think compartmentally about our lives. We believe some parts of life are sacred and some are secular. Our work is separate from our family, which is separate from our friends, and how we behave in one arena might look and feel quite different than how we behave in another. At its best, such fragmentation is unsettling; at its worse it can be outright dishonest.

The art of living a life of sacred intersections is itself a calling. Pursuing it in every aspect of your life, including your workplace, is a wonderful way to reintegrate an otherwise fragmented existence. It not only makes for a more rewarding life, it helps make your world—your *whole* world—a better place.

EIGHT: **COMMUNITY**

[purposeful unity and diversity]

Imagine if you had a group of friends with whom you regularly practiced sacred intersections. Imagine the trust and openness that would emerge if every time you saw those friends both you and they were aware of the intersection—occupied, mutually seeking each other's best, and fully engaged in knowing and enhancing each other's story. Imagine what it would be like to experience God's love together in that way, over an extended period of time. What would a community formed around sacred intersections look like?

Now imagine encouraging each other to find ways to live a life of sacred intersections for the benefit of others—not just for your group of friends. Imagine looking for opportunities to make a difference in your neighborhood or city and working together to accomplish it, each of you bringing your own best "profession" into the mix and feeding off of each other's strengths. Imagine planning a trip with some of those friends to serve victims or the poor or marginalized in a disadvantaged area of your city—perhaps even in another country. Imagine how meaningful those shared experiences would be.

And now think of the day when you and your friends are able to recount and celebrate those shared stories you created. Imagine the smiles on your faces—and on God's face—as you do.

That would be a pretty unique faith community, wouldn't it?

My guess is that all you've just imagined doesn't look a lot like most of the faith institutions you have encountered in your life. Why is it that most spiritually oriented organizations degrade into institutional forms over time, even when they began as a group of people passionately seeking to live out some altruistic goals?

Our natural desire for community is strong, but maintaining *authentic* community can be elusive. As individuals, we are relationally wired. (I think that's the core of the idea that we're made in the image of God. God is relational in essence and has implanted that into us as well.) Our sense of being and self-understanding are incomplete without relationships.

It is only in connection with others that we find ourselves.

That's what sacred intersections do for us. In accepting God's love, and in turn seeking to love others, we are getting our eyes off of ourselves and onto others. In losing ourselves we find freedom, and paradoxically, we find ourselves. And out of that experience, when intentionally practiced with others, community begins to form.

But there's a catch. The community that forms in this way feels wonderful at first, but it can easily turn back on itself. Once there's a perceived "us," that "us" can become the focus unless there is concerted effort to keep it from doing so. In the same way that I find myself by taking my eyes off of myself, true, sustainable spiritual community only finds itself as it gets its combined eyes off of itself. It must exist for the sake of others, or else it will become stagnant, even toxic.

Institution creeps in like this: When people form a group, it is typically because of some shared purpose or values. As those are lived out and enjoyed by the group, a sense of community forms and more people want to join in. As more people get involved, there is a natural push toward greater organization and the creation of defined programs. As these efforts become successful, even more people get involved, which leads to more organization and programming, which attracts more people, and so on.

As this cycle happens over time, the organization begins to take on a life of its own. Subtly at first, the priorities shift to dealing with issues related to the people involved. Increasing emphasis goes into designing and maintaining programs for those who are "in," rather than continually reevaluating, realigning and spreading out for the purposes around which the group originally formed. And then the "we're in, you're out" phenomena I describe in Chapter 3 begin to kick in, as the predicament of the knowledge of good and evil has its way. And when that happens, you have started down the road to institutionalizing—and the tail begins to wag the proverbial dog.

If things continue in that direction, some people will begin to derive their sense of identity and personal empowerment from the organization itself rather than the purposes behind the organization. You begin to notice certain people jockeying for positions that allow for greater influence—some with the best of intentions, others not. The power they gain is based on their position in the organization, and their energy is increasingly spent on preserving the organization.

Over time, positional power has a tendency to eat away at people. This doesn't always happen, but it's hard work to avoid it. It's all too easy to listen to your own press and develop delusions of grandeur. It's all too easy to lord it over people without fully hearing them or knowing them. It's all too easy to hide behind a position of power to do things that are harmful to others.

We are being barraged with reports of abuses of power in institutional settings—be they religious, educational, or political. And when such abuses are discovered, more often than not there was already an attempted cover-up intended to guard the institution's reputation. It's no wonder that such a prevailing cynicism has developed in western culture, especially among the young.

But it doesn't have to be that way. A purposeful community doesn't always have to become an institution, although a prevailing current flows in that direction and significant upstream energy is required to fight against it. Sacred intersections are a good source for that upstream energy, because they are, by nature, already other-focused. If community forms around a shared focus on others, it is much easier to stay that way corporately. When the heart of the community is for serving others, it cuts against the temptations of positional power.

Sacred intersections also inherently encourage inclusiveness. Diversity isn't a threat; it's a welcome friend. When we slow down in the intersections, infused with an assurance of God's love, we can listen to others' stories with an ear of understanding. When we encounter differences, we can be genuinely curious rather than judgmental, learn from each other, and actually *value* that those differences are there. Love that includes an appreciation of diversity is richer and deeper than that which is solely focused on similarity. Uniformity is a hollow substitute for unity.

When sacred intersections are the primary basis for unity, the power of diversity can be unleashed, as those involved bring out the best in each other for the sake of others. And that becomes contagious. Any time that two or more people who practice sacred intersections can serve the greater good alongside each other, it's amazing how others can then be drawn in.

You can easily observe this in the world of volunteering. "Serve the City" (STC) is a volunteer initiative that has flowed out of the organization I work with. STC seeks to address needs in the city by mobilizing volunteers to help existing non-profits and/or government agencies with the good work they are already doing. Many such agencies are undermanned, so an influx of helping hands is typically welcome. STC volunteers help those who are without homes, victims of domestic violence, elderly shut-ins, orphans, refugees, and many others. They might also serve by lifting people's spirits with a public art fair, a concert and picnic in the park, or by giving out free hugs in a busy plaza. Anyone can be an STC volunteer. Everyone is welcome. It's a way of declaring to the city that we're all in this together. One of the slogans of STC is, "We know them by their needs. What if we knew them by name?"[*]

---

[*] For more on Serve the City, go to www.servethecity.net

Interestingly enough, while those who are served are typically very appreciative of the help they receive, it is consistently those who do the serving that are most impacted. Helping someone in need has a way of breaking down barriers. The connections that happen are often profound, the conversations open, honest, and meaningful. People naturally want to be a part of something like that.

Philippe is a friend of mine in Montevideo, Uruguay. His parents divorced when he was young, and he was very independent during his teen years. Though he avoided serious trouble, he was often on the edge of it. Along the way, he met Matt, one of my colleagues who lives in Montevideo. They struck up bit of a relationship, but it faded over time. A few years ago, when Philippe was 19, he happened upon a Facebook posting from Matt about an upcoming, weeklong STC event in Montevideo. Philippe thought it sounded cool, so he wrote to see if he might be able to help on the opening day. Matt welcomed him, assigning him to be the host for a group of North American volunteers who were flying in for the week.

After the first day, Philippe made himself available for the rest of the week as well, and it had a profound impact on his life. It was the first time he had been around a group of people who were doing intentional acts of kindness together. He was captured by the stories of those people and the conversations he was having about life and God. By the end of the week, he knew he had found something worth keeping. Ever since, he has regularly been a part of STC in Montevideo, and now serves as one of the primary coordinators.

The friendships he made through volunteering with STC are the most important and meaningful in his life, and much to his liking, he is experiencing God at the center of those relationships. Philippe and his friends enjoy a faith community that is life-giving and counter-institutional. Their ongoing commitment to make a difference in their city enhances the open and honest love they have for each other.

Sadly, there seem to be too few faith communities that are like this. Instead, people today are leaving "organized religion" in droves, most often in reaction against institutional irrelevance and outright abuses.

While I applaud those anti-institutional sentiments, it grieves me that God is often thrown out along with the institution. It saddens me that he gets blamed for the abuses of institutional religiosity. (It's understandable that people would make such associations, because many within those institutions claim to be acting in God's name.)

Mostly I am dismayed that the fruit of the Tree of the Knowledge of Good and Evil has worked its way into humankind's religious strivings so deeply that it has caused us to create such distorted forms of institutional religiosity. It grieves me that these forms are so widely associated with God, when they are in fact so contrary to his nature.

More than anything, I want people to experience God in their lives. I want them to experience the freedom and wholeness that flow from his love.

I want them to experience the joy and meaning of connecting in authentic community with others, united in giving themselves to the well being of all, with God at the center of it.

Such community is transformative.

It can even be transformative enough to breathe fresh life back into a dying institution.

And when free of institutional baggage, this kind of community is the best vehicle there is for transporting the goodness of God. I would go so far as to say it is the hope of the world.

NINE: **REFLECTION**
[connecting it all back to God]

I am convinced that a life of sacred intersections is a beautiful, fulfilling way of living. I unashamedly invite people into it. I believe it will not only change them, but it will change their world. I have seen it happen in many people's lives.

It just works.

Which begs a question: Why?

For me, the most reasonable answer to that question is that living a life of sacred intersections must somehow be reflective of the nature of God. When we live that way, our stories fold into the story of God, and we sense him in it.

Please don't misunderstand me here. I'm not suggesting I have *the* definitive perspective on the nature of God or how he relates to the world. But I can say that what I have experienced in my own life, along with what I've observed in many others' lives, leads me to the above conclusion. Or at least it makes me think I'm onto something.

Now, to understand what I mean here, you need to know that when I use the phrase, "what I have experienced in my own life," there is more involved than simply my recollection of the events of my life. Everything in my life has taken place in contexts that were informed by many things, beginning with my cultural and religious heritage.

I don't claim to be unbiased. I don't think anyone can be completely unbiased.

But I have done a fair bit of reflecting on my own story and on how it has intersected with others' stories and with God. I've also had the privilege of making my profession in a passionate, caring non-profit organization that wrestles daily with many of these ideas and how they play out in peoples' lives.

I want to tell you how I gained the concepts I have shared in this book, because I hope that in hearing my process, it will help you to work your way through a similar process—one of considering your own story and heritage and how it all fits with the ideas presented in this book. If you have found truth and beauty in attempting to live out sacred intersections, then let that truth inform your understanding of your own story and perspectives.

Of course, there are challenges in trying to do this. Your story may include experiences that were similar to mine, but you drew different conclusions. Or perhaps my words will trigger some negative categories that you have developed. This may make it difficult for you to keep an open perspective. Nonetheless, I'll proceed with my story, with the hope that after having come this far in the book, you can treat this like any sacred intersection, slowing yourself down enough to listen without pre-judging.

I was raised in a loving family in a small city. We regularly attended a formal, liturgical church. Most of the language and ritual didn't make sense to me in my youth, nor did I then appreciate the beauty of the architecture, art, and music. For me, it was just something I had to do most Sundays.

In my high school years, I had my first encounters with people who talked openly about the Bible and about the life and teachings of Jesus without all the formal religious trappings. They spoke about God in relational terms. I was intrigued. I investigated it more and gradually began a long journey of seeking to follow Christ.

In the course of that journey—nearly 40 years now—I have been a part of several churches and had associations with several more. At times, I have found remarkable community with deep, meaningful relationships, and I have participated in many projects that made a positive impact on others' lives.

But, looking back, I also realize that I often unwittingly drifted along with others in the currents of institution. Much of our energy seemed to be focused inward. And even those programs intended for public service often had an ulterior motive: to get more people into the church—seemingly more for the church's sake than for the people's sake.

The motivation to draw people into a church can have subtle nuances, because if you are finding meaning and truth in a church setting, then you want others to experience it too. And that's good! It's just that it is really easy to begin thinking of people as targets. It's easy to start measuring success on how many people are showing up at events instead of on how effectively people's needs are being met. It's easy to start relying on simplistic "in-and-out" categories that don't reflect the complexity of each individual's story. And it's hard to keep on loving and serving people who aren't interested in your expression of church.

When there are strings attached, acts of service degrade into coercion.

It was about fifteen years ago when I began thinking about the implications of the knowledge of good and evil. Over time I realized, to my dismay, that much of what I was involved in was based on that knowledge. As I reevaluated, I began to see things that I had become desensitized to. I became more aware of spiritual smugness, posturing, politicizing, and outright judgmentalism—not just in hyper-fundamentalist churches, but also in the more common middle-of-the-road churches. All too often, it felt like the love and grace that Jesus represented was missing.

Also missing were the freedom and joy that flow out of love and grace, evidenced by rampant fear-based decision-making and legalistic manipulation—sometimes subtle, sometimes not so subtle.

And so I set about trying to reimagine what life would look like if lived beyond the knowledge of good and evil. I began to peel back the layers of institutionalism and fear in an effort to reconnect with the heart of things. I began to read the Bible differently, thinking more in terms of story and less in terms of dogma.

I was recaptured by the transcendent beauty and goodness of that story—the grand drama that unfolds over millennia—told through raw narrative, lavish poetry, rich allegory, personal letters of encouragement, and passionate prophecies, all of which reveal God's heart for us. It is the story of God pursuing us in order to restore what was lost when we chose the way of the knowledge of good and evil. It is God, in Jesus, tangibly entering into history's story to extend love, grace and forgiveness to each of us. And it is the story of him inviting us to join him as agents of that love, grace and forgiveness across all our categories and boundaries.

In my sacred intersections I find that story, and in that story I find the way of sacred intersections. They reflect each other. When I enter into another person's story, I am reminded that God has entered into my story. And when I experience God entering into my story, I am compelled to enter into others' stories. For me, at this point, they have become intertwined, and in that integration I find peace and joy and a greater capacity to love.

I now think of "church" as a community of people who practice sacred intersections. This can

happen in myriad ways, large or small, more structured or less structured, and even within a larger institutional framework. Whatever the context, I am
certain that this kind of community is life giving
and transformative. When we live as if God actually
loves us, it changes everything.

I don't know your story or heritage, so I'm not sure
how the concept of sacred intersections fits with
your cultural and religious perspectives. I can't
predict what layers, if any, you might have to peel
away in order to figure it out. You'll have to do that
work for yourself—and I hope you do. And if you
need help in doing it, may God guide you into intersections where you can find that help.

Whatever that process looks like in your life, my
hope is that it will end in a deeper awareness of
God's love for you and more of the freedom and
joy that come with it.

And may that propel you to a life filled with lovely,
fulfilling sacred intersections.

Through this book, you have had the opportunity to intersect a bit with my story.

I would love to intersect more with yours.

You can reach me at www.sacredintersections.net where you can also find additional resources, including a guide for further reflection and discussion.

ACKNOWLEDGMENTS

I am extremely grateful for the many people who helped make this book a reality. First, I am deeply indebted to the colleagues I've been alongside these past 20 years, learning, living out and encouraging the ideas presented herein.

I also want to thank all the people who have read and given helpful feedback on the manuscript in its various stages, with special thanks to Eric, Wes, Andrew, Rita, and Peter for going "above and beyond" with their thorough and insightful editorial input. And I'm so glad to have Bill Denzel's professional expertise in editing and production.

Thanks to Sascha, Roj, Teal, and Matthew for great conversations that added perspective and significantly helped to shape things. Thanks to Kevin, Dan & Shirley, and our own Sunday night friends, who have not only given feedback but have spent time discussing the book in group settings. Same goes to my Friday morning guys: thanks not only for your help with this book, but for being anchors in my life for years.

To all those who have made the final production of the book possible with their pledges on Kickstarter.com, thanks! Especially generous were Amer & Yvette, Dennis & Debi, Greg & Nancy, Julie, Mark & JoAnn, Neal & Kathy, Rob & Robi, Rodger & Carol, and Vendy.

It is difficult to determine how the influence of other writers works its way into one's own writing. Although there are undoubtedly others, I can say with certainty that you will find echoes of the following authors in this book: Bill Thrall, Bruce McNichol, and John Lynch; Parker Palmer; The Arbinger Institute; and Gregory Boyd. I am grateful to all of them for their influence in my life.

There are two special friends who have been uniquely helpful on every level with this book.

Thanks, Steve and Wil, for being alongside from inception to finish with your encouragement, insights, creativity, and practical input. Your friendship and support are invaluable to me.

And to my extended family: thanks for your love and support over the years. I owe much of who I am to all of you.

Lastly... Linda, Claire, and Maddie have not only been my biggest encouragers but also dedicated contributors to the process of creating this book. I love you so much and am eternally grateful that I get to have more sacred intersections with you than any other people on the planet.